THINGS

a Woman Must Know

22

THINGS

a Woman Must Know

IF SHE LOVES A MAN
WITH ASPERGER'S SYNDROME

Rudy Simone

Illustrated by Emma Rios

Jessica Kingsley Publishers
London and Philadelphia

First published in 2009
by Jessica Kingsley Publishers
73 Collier Street
London N19BE, UK
and
400 Market Street, Suite 400
Philadelphia, PA 19106, USA

www.jkp.com

Library of Congress Cataloging in Publication Data
A CIP catalog record for this book is available from the Library of Congress

British Library Cataloguing in Publication Data
A CIP catalogue record for this book is available from the British Library

ISBN 978 1 84905 803 2

Printed and bound in the United States by
Thomson-Shore, 7300 Joy Road, Dexter, MI 48130

To Bill

CONTENTS

FOREWORD

For over ten years I have worked with individuals and couples where one partner has Asperger Syndrome (AS). I have extensively researched the mental, emotional and physical effects that living in an AS/non-AS relationship can have on both partners. Research shows that more commonly, it is the man in the partnership who is affected by AS. I have frequently found that the women in the relationship work in the caring profession and are by nature very nurturing, caring and highly empathic. It appears that this type of woman is attracted to the seemingly child-like qualities that a man with AS will portray. This works initially in the relationship but over time, due to the neurological impact having AS will cause, the woman may start to feel her empathic ways are not being reciprocated. She may begin to feel emotionally isolated along with a sense of loneliness, and become aware that something is missing in the relationship. If the reasons for this are not identified then the long term stress this can cause will result in what is termed 'Cassandra Affective Deprivation Disorder' (CADD). Of course, this emotional deprivation is not the intention of the AS partner; it is due to the limitations of theory of mind caused by having AS. However, if AS is not recognized, then neither partner will be aware of the cause and this will often result in blaming and frustration.

The majority of adults affected by AS will also be affected by Alexithymia, which is a Greek word meaning 'no words for feelings'. Research has now shown that being in a relationship with a partner with Alexithymia will negatively affect relationship satisfaction and quality. The effects of this, and CADD, can be reduced if both partners accept and understand what is responsible for the difficulties in communication, intimacy and empathy within the relationship; it is then more likely that problems and misunderstandings can be avoided.

Men with AS are capable of true love, but as Rudy points out, the woman may not feel she is being loved in quite the way she would have hoped for. Often in the beginning of an AS/non-AS relationship, the female partner may have felt that she was the centre of his attention and been very flattered by the devotion and consideration he showed her. He will have made her feel very special and in some cases flooded her with time, gifts and romantic gestures. This passionate, initial stage can end quite quickly and once they marry or live together it can come to rather an abrupt end; she will be left wondering what went wrong or worse still, what did she do wrong. The relationship will then for her enter a stage of hope, where she will often begin in 'rescuer mode'; then when nothing changes and the distance and lack of attention increases, she will find herself switch into 'persecutor mode'. This is where her own self loathing starts to build up as she finds herself not liking the person she is becoming. How she acts and behaves will also have a huge impact on him. He will rarely make the connection between his behavior and her reactions. He will interpret her words as criticism and believe that she is saying he is a failure or has got it wrong again, whilst he truly believes that he is doing his best.

There are many books that have been written about being in a relationship with a man with AS, but I have found none to be as insightful, accurate and understanding of both perspectives as this book by Rudy Simone. Each section of the book says it just the way it is; it is realistic, positive and unbiased.

If you are in an AS/non-AS relationship or embarking on a relationship with a man with AS, then this book will give you all the information and advice you need to avoid this 'cycle' from happening. The book does not suggest that anyone should tolerate abuse in a relationship, but points out that sometimes it is necessary to work out what behavior is due to AS and what is not. Having AS does not make a person physically or verbally abusive; that is down to personality and the person with AS has control over this.

This book highlights the difficulties that can arise in a relationship due to the male partner having AS, and this can be regardless as to whether the female partner also has AS; my research has shown the effect on her can be the same. Rudy illustrates how these difficulties can be avoided and what positives a woman can take from them. She has achieved this in an unique, realistic and professional way that will soon become essential reading for any woman in love with a man affected by Asperger syndrome.

Maxine Aston, Author of 'The Other Half of Asperger Syndrome', 'Aspergers in Love' and 'The Asperger Couples Workbook'.

Introduction

Asperger's syndrome (AS) is an autism spectrum disorder, but the condition is much less visible and apparent than classic autism. It is not so much a disability as a *diff*ability. People with AS are often brilliant in some respects, but they may display different social and emotional responses than what is considered the norm. Some individuals with AS are more obviously affected, while others are not, and may go most or all of their life without being properly diagnosed (Barnhill 2004). AS is not a psychological condition, it is neurological—the result of different "wiring" in the brain. People with AS are individuals and no two exhibit the same variety or intensity of traits. But, nearly all of them will find one area of life more challenging than others—the area of romantic relationships.

This challenge will be strongest because it involves communication, expectation, and socialization as well as sensory issues, all problematic for a person with AS. And, because they sometimes need to retreat and rejuvenate from a world which is constantly confusing to them, periods of solitude are an almost universal requirement for those with AS. Consequently, close cohabitation with another human being is difficult; not just for them but for those they live with.

This book is directed mainly toward female partners of men with AS; to discuss *what* problems they will likely encounter, and *why*. It will provide some insight into *his* thoughts on those issues, and illuminate or remind us of the positive aspects of loving someone with AS.

Why is this book necessary? If you are in a relationship with an AS male, feelings of emotional deprivation and self-doubt can set in, resulting in what is known as *Cassandra Affective deprivation Disorder* (CAD). CAD is a condition of depression and ill health that comes from the isolation and loneliness of *knowing* the truth about something or someone, *experiencing* that truth, but not being believed. This book may help you avoid or alleviate that condition by letting you know that what you are going through has been experienced by other women, and offering some practical advice where possible.

Some have claimed CAD doesn't exist, that it is merely depression in women who have an unhappy love life or who are rejected and want to blame Asperger's and their partner for the failure of the relationship. Other neurological, psychological, and behavioral conditions didn't "exist" until someone gave them a name, and many have denied things such as attention deficit hyperactivity disorder (ADHD) with the same dismissiveness. Syndromes are just clusters of symptoms hanging around together, and which we name, just as we draw lines between stars and call them constellations; it is easier to say "big dipper" than to name each of its stars individually. Whether or not you agree that CAD stands as a legitimate disorder doesn't matter so much. What does seem to matter is that so many women in love with AS men experience many of the same doubts, have the same questions, and share very similar experiences, frustrations, and symptoms. For the sake of simplicity, if not science, we will use the term CAD when referring to this unique situation. If the term bothers you, think of the acronym as standing for "Confused And Depressed."

According to Aston (2008) the symptoms of CAD are similar to seasonal affective disorder (SAD) and/or affection deprivation disorder (ADD), and include:

- low self-esteem

- feeling confused/bewildered

- feelings of anger, depression, and anxiety

- feelings of guilt

- loss of self/depersonalization

- phobias—social/agoraphobia

- posttraumatic stress reactivity

- breakdown.

Possible psychosomatic effects include:

- fatigue

- sleeplessness

- migraines

- loss or gain in weight

- premenstrual tension (PMT)/female-related problems

- myalgic encephalomyelitis (ME)

- low immune system—resulting in anything from colds to cancer.

So why don't these women just leave if they've got it so bad? Matters of the heart are not that simple and most of the women I've talked to were deeply in love with their AS man, despite problems. They were not looking to blame, but merely wanted to make things better. While many of these women were not displaying significant symptoms of CAD, all of them were looking for ways to connect with their partner on a deeper level, and their inability to do so was causing them varying amounts of frustration and pain.

The information in this book was taken mainly from three things:

- my own personal experience

- interviews with men and women who contacted me via my website (www.help4aspergers.com)

- forums I joined specifically for people with or affected by AS.

From these three sources I compiled a list of traits, problems, and solutions—or at least healthy coping skills.

I asked the men their opinion on some of the many common issues couples were facing. Because difficulty talking about emotions is an Aspergian trait, it was often easier to get their views on a *topic* or an *event*, rather than asking them direct questions about their own feelings and actions. Some were able to talk openly about their own past actions and intentions. I have put relevant quotes from these conversations and responses into a section called "*His words*," which may be found in each chapter.

All details which could potentially be used to identify someone have been changed or omitted, but the gist of each story or viewpoint is intact and accurate. I think it is worth mentioning that this book is not about AS females as a group, but it appears that AS women, if they are in a relationship with an AS male, can and often do experience the same problems as neurotypical (NT) women (Aston 2005), including CAD.

When I finally sat down to write this book an image arose in my mind—that an Asperger man is like a rock and the woman who loves him is water, molding herself around him. As a rock is shaped by water, he will be shaped by her influence, but ever so slowly. She will be better off being gentle and persistent, for, if she comes on strong like a wave, she'll only break herself upon his immovable frame time and again until there is nothing left of her and she is spent.

The purpose of this book is definitely *not* to disparage men with Asperger's nor is it to discourage the women who love them. For along with challenges, the syndrome carries with it unique gifts and wonderful traits that are not mentioned in any diagnostic manuals. But these relationships stand a better chance of success if each party knows what they're getting into. Whether you are newly dating, in a long-term relationship, or if you're married to a man with Asperger's, this book can help you. If you're an AS male this book can assist you in understanding your female partner; to see your behavior from her point of view. I have tried to put things forward in an honest manner, without putting a too-positive spin on them. And, of course, these are generalizations, even if they are gleaned from specific instances and testimonies, and I stress: *not all of them will apply to everyone.* I apologize in advance for generalizing, but it cannot be helped in something like this.

If you are the partner of a man with Asperger's you may be the one who first noticed his anomalies; he may or may not be officially diagnosed. You might be perpetually frustrated at your inability to connect with him on a deep and consistent level. One day you feel as if your relationship is finally on solid ground, and the next day that ground has dropped out from under you. You may be wondering if you are the only woman in the world who is feeling what you are feeling. You're not.

Women in love with Asperger men tend to be smart, capable women who like challenge in a relationship. But even so, it may be more of a challenge at times than you bargained for. If you are seeking romantic fulfillment in traditional form, there can be a certain amount of emotional danger in this relationship, an inherent risk.

This book is meant to minimize that risk, help you surmount these challenges, and increase the possibility of a successful and healthy relationship.

1

There will be
loneliness

No matter how much your AS male loves you, there will be numerous times and ways that he cannot connect with you. Whether he needs to be alone physically or is just emotionally distant, be warned—this will happen. You must try not to take it personally. Social withdrawal, adherence to strict routines, and sensory overload, all symptoms of Asperger's, will cause him to "retreat" on a more or less frequent basis. He will probably have difficulty compromising on this. Even if you made agreements in advance, for example, to spend a certain amount of time together, he may try to bend those terms his way. He may see your desire to spend more time with him with as weakness on your part, and his need to be alone as strength and independence, especially if he is undiagnosed or hasn't quite come to terms with having AS. If you demand more time from him, or more closeness, you may be accused of being "clingy" or needy. As with every other situation in this book, if he truly loves you (and that may not be clear), then he has to be willing to compromise. But so do you. For without compromise, you will both burn out.

This may surprise you to hear if you are in the early stages of your relationship. An Aspie can and does often go the other way, inviting himself over too much, overstaying his welcome. But soon he will tire of the constant company and you may not see or hear from him for a while. If you call him he might not answer the phone or ring back right away. He is getting the peace and time to regenerate that he requires. If you are looking for a partner who will be joined to you at the hip 24/7, then you will have to readjust your expectations, otherwise you are almost sure to be disappointed.

Meanwhile, he may not even be aware of the hurt that this is causing you. One of the main difficulties in

Asperger's is understanding one's own and others' emotions. If he can't understand his own emotions, how can he possibly understand yours? The more you try to explain, the more confused and withdrawn he might become.

Although he may be there physically, there might be a silence or an emotional distance between you that leaves you feeling lonely and cold. He cannot help it: it may sound like a contradiction, but this seeming insensitivity actually stems in part from oversensitivity. People with AS can get sensory overload quite easily, causing confusion, which can lead to emotional and physical shutdown. He will be quiet and in his own world from time to time whether you are there or not. This sensitivity also extends to the physical—you might think cuddling on the couch watching a movie is a great idea but he would find that extremely uncomfortable and will probably sit at the far end of the sofa from you if you let him. If you are new to the world of AS this kind of thing can really hurt and cause you to question why on earth he's there with you, since he doesn't seem to notice or want you. Trust this: if he is there with you, then chances are he wants to be. He probably finds your presence comforting and reassuring even if he hasn't got a clue how to express it.

One of the most important things that you have to take on board is this: although you may quite easily accept that your man sometimes needs, physically and emotionally, to retreat from the world, you must understand that he'll also need to retreat from you.

HIS WORDS

"I didn't call my girlfriend for a few days. She had abandonment issues and broke up with me."

"My girlfriend and I are both Aspies. We both need to spend time alone and are perfectly happy seeing each other twice a week."

WHAT TO DO

If you do not live together, pace yourselves in the relationship, and space your visits out, so that burn-out doesn't happen. Remember that his need for alone time is usually not personal or a reflection on your relationship. Discuss minimizing distractions when you are together, such as turning off phones, staying off computers and televisions, and making an effort to do things together.

If you do live together, respect his need for space and privacy, allow him his shutdowns, and don't be confrontational or critical when he is emotionally withdrawn; it will only push him further inward.

THE POSITIVE NOTE

You have a unique opportunity—you'll have the independence of a single woman, space, and time to pursue your own interests. You'll retain the strength that comes from standing on your own two feet while still enjoying many of the perks of having a steady partner.

2

There will probably
be no public displays
of affection

If you are the kind of woman who likes to hold hands on the street, or kiss on a beach at sunset, dating an Aspie is not for you. They are (generally) notoriously opposed to any public displays of affection, even public touching of any sort. Although you may think this is not a big deal, it becomes a big deal when your man refuses to hold you when you feel affectionate. It feels like deprivation and rejection, and both those things can resonate with early childhood scars and/or create new ones.

This may also happen in private. Some men say they don't like the feel of holding hands. Physical sensation is highly sensitized for an AS person. Some are so sensitive that even eye contact can "hurt," while others just don't see the point of kissing and hugging.

As with other things in this book, there may be an incident in his past that left an emotional scar, in this case one related to public affection. One man intimated that his best friend saw him kissing his girlfriend and then that friend stole the girlfriend from him. A neurotypical (NT) psyche might realize that was an isolated incident, but the AS mind may see that as an inevitable outcome to any similar display.

He may even think your wanting to hold hands in the mall is a way to advertise *your* desirability. Although there is often a grain or more of truth in that logic, he probably doesn't see that spontaneous affection and physical touch is just a normal human need. He might know it intellectually, but not be able to put it into practice.

On the other hand, and most annoyingly, your man may behave inappropriately toward other women right in front of you, i.e. flirt, not realizing that this could be misconstrued and hurtful. He may just be trying to affirm to himself that he is a desirable man, or he may not be aware that he's doing it. Since he probably is faithful, he can't imagine why or how you could possibly be jealous. (By the admission of many AS men, they don't know how to flirt or cheat even if they wanted to and an overwhelming majority believe in fidelity.)

When you try to explain to him that this is hurtful, he may accuse *you* of insecurity, rather than seeing his own behavior as inappropriate. He doesn't see the disparity between his coolness toward you in public and his warmth toward others, so is confounded as to how it could bother you.

HIS WORDS

On kissing:

> "I only like kissing when I'm having sex, otherwise it bugs me."

> "I don't understand the significance of it."

On flirting:

> "If the relationship is strong, then there is no need for the woman to feel insecure. If I am being nice to another girl in front of you, then I have nothing to hide. I'm nice to everyone, regardless of gender. There should be no genders."

WHAT TO DO

You must learn to become secure in your own desirability. Insecurity will not serve you. That said, not receiving the spontaneous affection you crave can still be hard to take. Try to get him to compromise, a little at a time. Sneak a kiss at sunset, or hold hands when no one can see. Make a game of it.

THE POSITIVE NOTE

It is possible that your man may only be able to let his guard completely down when he is alone with you.

THE POSITIVE NOTE

You can be sure that saying "I love you" is not nearly as meaningful as putting those words into actions. If your man truly does love you, you probably have evidence all around if you look for it. You will learn to value actions over words.

4

He will take you
and the relationship
for granted

Just when you start to feel comfortable, like your relationship has made progress, and you're getting closer as a couple, he may become bored. This can happen early on, and it can happen again and again. Apathy with regard to all friendships is common among people with AS. They don't usually take the initiative to call or maintain contact. But it is much easier to take this personally if you're his girlfriend, rather than just his friend. He will show this boredom in any number of ways—not calling, being cold when you call or see him, looking blatantly at other women in front of you, criticizing you, and so on. There is no easy way to handle this, and this is often the point where many relationships end (for the first time or one of many times). Of course, you can tell him his behavior is hurting you, but at this point, he probably won't care. He is deeply entrenched in the "I don't want to be in a relationship" phase that often passes.

It seems that one reason women put up with this (i.e. don't leave or try to keep the relationship together) is because it often happens out of the blue and doesn't seem like part of any natural progression. In other words, the couple might have their best week ever, and then he suddenly goes cold. Although at some point he has to decide that he truly wants to be with you, it seems common for AS men to get cold feet several times in the relationship.

When asked, some men admit that they do get easily bored with their girlfriends after the discovery period is over. Some say that they have acted in such a way as to make the girl break up with them, rather than taking the responsibility themselves to end things. Of those, some thought it would be "less hurtful for her" if she did the breaking up, while others knew they were being cruel but didn't care, which suggests there's a certain emotional detachedness going on at the time. Later on, some of those men came to believe they'd made a mistake and went back with their partner.

Most men with AS claim that they are very sincere. Of course, men and women always have had difficulty understanding each other's motives, and both teams have accused the other of game-playing. Whatever you want to call it, the usual games of relationships are intensified. For example, when a woman's phone call goes unanswered and unreturned for a while, she might think he's playing a mind game, when in actuality he just doesn't feel like talking. Some AS men have said women "led them on for a couple of weeks and then dumped them," rather than seeing them as having tried and failed to get the response they needed.

One thing appears to be clear: women in relationships with AS males have to be clever. You have to navigate choppy waters, and that requires vigilance, planning, and occasionally consulting the stars. Unfortunately, this may be construed by him as conspiring. One woman was accused of constantly "plotting" to trap her man, when she was just tap-dancing to try and keep him happy and the relationship together. Your best efforts may get very little back, and they may get little appreciation.

Don't assume just because he's quiet and uncomplaining that he's content. He can just up and go without warning and tell you afterward that he was bored.

HIS WORDS

"I definitely get bored with people, girlfriends included. But Aspies don't like change much, so I might stay even if I don't really want to."

"A lot of Aspies don't realize how much work it takes to keep a relationship going and they get lazy."

"He may be trying to get rid of you (if he stops calling or starts acting like a jerk) but isn't mature enough to tell you."

WHAT TO DO

Many women say it is better if they stop calling him completely when he gets like this; then he becomes intrigued again and may make an effort to call or try harder to please you. Provided you still love him, you will probably want to do something to pique his interest from time to time. But don't go to extremes by changing yourself, such as dye your hair, plastic surgery, etc. (hey, some women do), because he will only get bored with that too. Or he'll tell you afterward that he liked you better the way you were before.

Stop playing those games if it doesn't serve you to do so. It does take effort to be in a relationship with an Aspie—most will agree with that. You may be better off coming from a place of sincerity, and relaxing your efforts a little, so you don't exhaust yourself and get tied up in mental knots. Chances are, he will feel your tension if you're trying too hard.

THE POSITIVE NOTE

You will not become complacent. You will constantly be challenged from within and without to be creative, to find new ways to keep romance alive. But, by taking what comes and observing, you will let the relationship unfold more naturally.

Many women say that they enjoy the challenge of dating their AS male; that they get bored with an easy relationship. This won't be boring.

5

He may have a more
patient approach to sex
than you do

Many men with AS say that they are celibate or asexual, either out of choice or because they can't find or maintain a relationship. Some NT women have a "relationship" with an AS male that is without sexual intercourse, by the man's choice.

Although men with AS are usually perfectly capable of pleasing their women, some say that they are unable to completely let themselves go in the act—they get distracted by sights, sounds, and so on. One man had to stop midway and floss his teeth because they were bothering him. There are sensory issues—they need to feel the right fabrics and smell the right smells. This can be true for NTs as well of course, but, in his case, it's more pronounced. He may also be emotionally detached while having sex, while you are in the throes of love and passion.

Prior emotional hurts can make an AS male much more cautious about getting involved sexually with a woman, and of course, once you cross that line, there are "expectations" and it can't be reiterated enough how uncomfortable an AS male can be with those.

Some men say that to feel comfortable with either cuddles or sex they need to feel very relaxed; that the best way to this state is a massage, rather than eye contact, words, or handholding. A firm massage is preferable to light touch, which many find annoying and uncomfortable.

While many of the women interviewed were happy with the sex they have with their AS partner, it can be infrequent. One woman said her AS male was so sensitive he "convulsed" every time she touched him and they were quite sexually active after three years. One of the most seemingly contented NT women had no sex at all with her male; he couldn't handle the complication of a sexual relationship but she accepts that and maintains that they are in every other way a couple. She enjoys sex but cannot fathom seeking it from anyone else.

HIS WORDS

"Because of these sharp overactive senses I can't let myself go during sex like NTs do."

WHAT TO DO

There does seem to be a consensus that AS males need to be very relaxed. Learn to give a good firm back-rub. If he doesn't want to have sex with you, then it is entirely up to you whether you can live with that or not. If sex is very important to you, you may have to consider having a friendship with him and looking elsewhere for romance.

A word of caution: Don't fall in to the trap of thinking you are not behaving at your "highest" when things he does (or doesn't do) bother you. Romantic relationships are meant to fulfill emotional and physical needs, as well as practical ones.

THE POSITIVE NOTE

If you aren't getting as much as you like, at least you know he's not just there for the sex! And, you'll have more time for other things.

6

Communication
will always be
a challenge

He will always find it difficult to tell you how he feels and what he wants. In return, he will always have a hard time hearing about how you feel, for many AS men just don't know what to say.

Although people with AS have varying degrees of verbal skills and eloquence, Alexithymia (difficulty in experiencing, expressing, and describing emotional responses) is a key component of AS (Fitzgerald and Molyneux 2004). At the same time that he is grappling with being unable to access his own inner emotional life, he is unable to process what you are saying about yours: he gets confused by eye contact, tone, and other things he has a hard time understanding. This confusion and frustration can cause him to clam up, walk away, and try to avoid any future conversations about feelings. It can also make him defensive, where even the gentlest talk about your emotions or the relationship may be viewed as an attack or criticism of his character.

The problems in communication will not stop there.

LYING

Your man may not always tell the truth or the whole story. While at times he will be brutally honest, on other occasions you will get the sense you're not hearing the whole truth. Your Aspie's logic will differ from the norm. There may be things he says and does that in his mind are rational and just, but to your eyes, will be less than honest. His moral compass won't always point "north." He may not tell the whole truth if it's not in his best interest, or if he thinks it's not in yours. Or, rather than telling a lie, he may be evasive or vague.

Although Attwood (2007) often describes AS as "the

pursuit of knowledge, truth, and perfection," and I do agree with that statement, it has been admitted by some Aspies that they are good liars, but that they only tell white lies that don't hurt anyone. A person with AS often has an ability greater than their education and some have disclosed "fibbing" their way into jobs because they knew they could do the work even though they didn't have the degree or education.

One AS male says that he lies to get out of social situations without embarrassment. When he gets uncomfortable and wants to leave a place, he won't say "I have AS and can be uncomfortable with people," he'll say "I have a stomach-ache," or something similar. Whether they have lied to get a good job, or to avoid embarrassment, it has worked for them in the past, so it may have become a habit. Habits are not shaken off so easily. Maturity, education, diagnosis, and acceptance all seem to have a bearing on how honest he is.

DEFENSIVENESS

Another common problem in communication is defensiveness. This may be at least partly attributed to the fact that many people with AS are bullied all their lives, usually from adolescence on. So even the gentlest attempts at reasoning may at first hit a wall of self-protectiveness. He's been used to being misunderstood and misrepresented all his life. (Being a square peg constantly trying to fit into a round hole and possibly being mocked or condemned for it.)

His defensiveness can be brought about in numerous ways. One way is by telling him your needs are not being met in the relationship; he may see this as an unprovoked attack. Also, people with AS are usually very intelligent and can, by their own admission, be know-it-alls. If you are questioning him, his activities, or his motives, this will almost certainly make him defensive.

BLAMING

Defensiveness can lead to blaming. They may blame you for something that is their own (or no one's) fault, just because you are there. One woman told how her man illegally passed a car on the right. The driver was making a right hand turn and he smashed into her passenger side door. Instead of taking responsibility for his actions, he told the police that she didn't have her blinker on, that she stopped suddenly, and he had to swerve to the right (which was not true). He also yelled at his wife and their passenger for talking while he was driving, saying it distracted him. The accident was entirely his fault but he blamed everyone else, including the cop that gave him the resultant ticket.

Using the word "fault" is common. There's a scene in "Mozart and the Whale," a film about two characters with Asperger's, where the main character, Donald, tells his prospective employer that it is his girlfriend's "fault" that he is there for the job. He blames her rather than giving her credit (Lawrence and Naess 2005).

Some AS men, especially undiagnosed ones, will often blame the difficulties in the relationship upon their partner. As one man told me, "women attracted to Aspies come with their own set of issues." If the woman internalizes that blame, this is another trigger for the onset of CAD, which is partly caused by an erosion of self-esteem and an increase in self-doubt.

Diagnosed men are much more likely to take at least half the responsibility for difficulties and are less likely to see her questions or words as attacks and criticisms.

Blaming and defensiveness, dishonesty, and a general lack of verbal skills in some people with AS all make for communication challenges. Though many with Asperger's can be quite eloquent when they want to, they may have a mind-set of "why bother" since they feel they're not going to be heard anyway. His silence may not be voluntary: some with AS report intermittent breakdowns in their ability to speak (selective mutism), particularly when confronted or scolded.

HIS WORDS

"I never know what to say."

On lying:

"Aspies have to lie to get by."

"Since they can have guilty body language even when they're not lying, they get accused of it anyway."

On blame:

"My first girlfriend was a liar and my second girlfriend was a psycho ... they destroyed the relationship with their messed up ways."

"All the relationships I've had have fallen apart but it wasn't my fault."

WHAT TO DO

People with AS love to learn. If a subject is broached intellectually rather than emotionally you have a better chance of getting him to hear you. Practice the fine art of conversation without expectation. People will open up easier if they feel they're not being pressured. If he senses an ulterior motive he'll clam up. If you are the sort of person who really likes to talk about feelings and relationships, learn to talk about other things: places, events, science, art, and so on.

One way to aid communication, or at least to tell him how you feel, is to put it in a letter. Many men say that they like to receive cards and letters from their partner. It gives them time to process the words, without getting confused by all those non-verbal things that are a distraction.

As for honesty, try to be compassionate and patient. Teach by example. Because of the challenges of having AS, as stated, they may have had to adopt some shifty behaviors to survive. Use humor when possible to open the door to conversation and choose your battles wisely.

THE POSITIVE NOTE

Your own conversational and listening skills will be improved. You can be instrumental in strengthening his conversational skills and his level of honesty, if it needs it.

7

There will be shock

No matter how much you know about Asperger's there will always be situations where your man is so insensitive that it shocks you. Literal, physical, and emotional shock. That is because you think deep down he understands you better than he really does. You may also think you know him better than you really do. He will put himself first, and this can manifest at the strangest of times.

One woman's partner invited her to a club, then left her there all alone because he got in a "bad mood" and took a bus home. She was humiliated, hurt, and angered, all the more so because this was a holiday and they had a history of not spending them together. This was to be, in her eyes, a milestone in their relationship; his way of acknowledging her as his girlfriend. Even though he'd left places before because of his social discomfort he'd never left her behind. The fact the he left her alone among hundreds of drinking, dancing, celebrating strangers showed a flagrant disregard for her feelings and her personal safety. She felt abandoned and it was too much for her to take. She felt that if he could do this, he could not be relied upon at all. She ended the relationship.

All the things that attracted you to your man—his gentleness, his boyish charm, will not prepare you for this sort of behavior. People with AS have to be actors—*good* actors—to try and fit in with society, so he may keep his anomalies hidden for a while. But after a time, AS behaviors will come out, and they may do so suddenly, without warning, and it may be something that completely surprises you.

Some AS men can be brutal in the way they end a relationship. One man said he left his girlfriend of two years without warning and without a word. He claimed he really didn't know how much he was hurting her at the time.

Another woman related how she'd been dating her man and it was love at first sight. They were very close almost immediately. One night, just a couple of weeks into their relationship, he became quite sullen, and went and sat on her porch alone. When she came out to see what he was up to, he told her to leave him alone. When she asked what was wrong, he told her to "shut up." Bear in mind, they'd had no argument, and it was her house. She became frightened that he was schizophrenic and potentially dangerous. It was quite a shock for her to see her sweet man behave this way. He was undiagnosed at this point and this was the first real indication that there was something "abnormal" going on inside him.

Situations like this will shake you up and test the strength of your feelings. These kinds of extreme behaviors will indicate that he needs a diagnosis if he hasn't had one, and if he has had one, that he hasn't quite taken it on board. If he is behaving in such a way, he's not doing enough to try and manage his own behavior and/or is still not entirely cognizant of his effect on others. He may need some help. If he is in the early stages of acceptance and management of AS, he will probably blame you rather than himself or AS. Rejection of him at this point will only confirm in his mind, that you were not right for him.

HIS WORDS

"I didn't know how erratic and hurtful I was toward her until mutual friends told me I was acting like a sociopath."

"How I handle situations isn't just Asperger's, it depends on my upbringing and education."

"Looking back I can see how I might have hurt her. I handle things differently since I've been diagnosed."

WHAT TO DO

Hold steady. You know he has AS, or at least you suspect it, or you wouldn't be reading this book. Try to remember that his behavior has nothing to do with you. It comes from within, and from his perception of the current situation. If you remain calm, you will have a greater chance of him hearing you than if you get upset and confrontational. Take things in your stride and try not to see every slight as a crisis. Try to persuade him to seek help and/or a diagnosis. Do not blame yourself.

THE POSITIVE NOTE

You will probably see that he recovers from these situations a lot more easily than you do. He won't cling to a drama. Perhaps you can learn to do the same, by approaching solutions logically rather than reacting emotionally.

8

Your man may not
be there for you
in a crisis

A man with AS can be altruistic, helpful, and, at times, positively heroic. Yet, when he is "expected" to come through for someone, he may not be able to handle it. For example, one man refused to visit his aunt after she'd had a stroke though she asked for him daily (they were close, at least in her eyes). He wouldn't even admit to himself that she'd had a stroke or that she might not survive. It was busy season in his work and he didn't have time to spare, especially when he believed she'd be home again soon anyway. It can be hard to maintain respect for him in the face of such behavior.

Again, this has to do with pressure, expectations, drama, and all the other things that can tie an AS man up in knots. He knows he will feel, and therefore be, ineffectual. So, he thinks, "Why bother?" He may feel that there are other people, e.g. doctors, lawyers, your mother, and so forth, who are better equipped to handle whatever crisis it is that you are going through. It won't occur to him that you might just find his presence comforting and that he doesn't have to *do* or *say* anything.

If the crisis in question is a relationship crisis, he will probably be at a total loss as to what he did wrong, or what the problem is, and may think you are being a neurotic drama queen. Tears in such a context will probably be met with defensiveness and incomprehension. The more dramatic the outburst, the more likely he is to shut down and stop communicating completely, or just walk away.

HIS WORDS

"It wasn't a big deal."

"I thought about calling her, but I didn't know

what to say. I mean, what could I possibly do to help?"

WHAT TO DO

If you are hurt or injured, physically or emotionally, and he isn't the one that helps you, try to remember this: he is there for you, presumably, in so many other ways, there will be times you will have to depend on others to assist you in your time of need.

THE POSITIVE NOTE

You will learn to rely on others and not just on your man. Many women do look to their partner for so many things and that can wear down even the healthiest of relationships, putting undue pressure on one person to be all for another. This knowledge will keep you connected with the world.

9

Many AS males can
be cranky, or have bad
tempers, and can explode
at the slightest of things

Although he may be gentle and calm much of the time, he can have an absolute conniption fit if he can't find the right hammer or someone forgot to put the cheese on his burger.

This behavior is usually not violent, but can be hyperbolic and inappropriate to the situation. He can be crass or hostile at these times, and he may even tell you to "shut up" or curse a lot. Emotionally he is probably not as mature as his age, and may handle frustration like a child.

One woman told me her man was very nice to all his customers, was well-liked by them, and noted for his gentle and kind behavior. But this same man could be really hostile to people that upset him, especially cashiers. It happened on several occasions that they displeased him and he became very rude: insulting, yelling, screeching his tires out of drive-throughs, etc. This behavior embarrassed and confused her, because his reaction was out of proportion to the inciting incident.

Some men with AS, by contrast, are usually calm and good-natured. Besides upbringing and education, this may have something to do with diagnosis. If you suspect your man has AS but he hasn't been diagnosed, or if he has been diagnosed but hasn't taken time to research and understand it, he will have no frame of reference for a lot of his emotional and social difficulties. This can result in frustration which may vent itself through angry outbursts. Knowing what the culprit is (AS) can make him stop and think before reacting; it can put things in perspective. It will enable him to say "I have Asperger's. That's why this is hard for me." This can take some of the burden off.

On the other hand, some have said that diagnosis made them deteriorate, and their symptoms stronger. They didn't feel like trying to be "normal" any more since they knew they never could be anyway. Finding out they had AS made them rage against the world, and angry that it wasn't detected sooner. That is why early detection is important and follow-up support is necessary, as is more understanding of the syndrome in general.

A word of caution: a diagnosis *is* important. But while the possibility for accurate diagnosis of autism using the *DSM-IV* is excellent, the accuracy of diagnosis for Asperger's using the manual has come under question (Attwood 2003). In addition, detection in adults can be much more complicated than in children; they've had many years to unlearn tics and learn new tricks for fitting in. To ensure accurate diagnosis, try to find a doctor that is an expert; one who truly understands *adult* Asperger's and knows what to look for.

HIS WORDS

"I'm a lot better since I got the diagnosis. I don't get so angry because I know it's AS; it's not me or her, or them."

"I think that my diagnosis was withheld from me for a long time. I should have been told sooner."

WHAT TO DO

Encourage him to get that piece of paper, for his own peace of mind. By all means, keep your sense of humor. When he is blowing up over nothing, don't add fuel to the fire by blowing up at him. Try to look at things from his point of view. When the incident is over and you are both calm, ask him what he meant or what his perspective was at the time. You may find his point of view enlightening. If you're still convinced his behavior was inappropriate, try to put it to him logically, perhaps putting him on the receiving or observing end of the behavior or scenario. He may begin to see that his behavior was not desirable or considerate. But be patient, altering one's perception of reality takes time, and so does learning new behavior.

Sometimes a person with AS can get into a dangerous situation because of their temper—meaning they can make someone so angry that they provoke an attack. Often people with AS have no idea of the effect they're having on others and cannot sense when they are entering into a danger zone. Try to make him see the potential hazards of losing his temper. You might suggest taking up some form of anger management (e.g. meditation, or something more physical like running) in addition to the diagnosis.

THE POSITIVE NOTE

As with other incidents, your man may recover his good humor almost as quickly as he lost it. Observe how he doesn't hang on to things. It can be absolutely inspiring.

Depression can be anger turned inward. If he is letting off steam as it comes, as long as he isn't violent (and men with AS usually aren't), it is probably better than if he keeps it in where it will turn on him.

10

Your man may have a hard time completing a college degree, holding on to a job, or seeing things through

There are many reasons this may be the case, but social anxieties are probably at the top of the list. As already stated, many people with AS have been bullied from adolescence. The effect of this can be justified wariness, because bullying is not just a distant memory for adults with AS—it can and often does occur in offices and college classrooms as much as playgrounds. Social groups have their pecking order and, of course, it's those who lack social skills or who are different that get picked on the worst.

Difficulty holding a job or completing a degree also has to do with trying to function as an AS in a world designed for and by NTs. The physical, mental, emotional, and social expectations are all foreign to the AS mind. The "physical" things can include tangibles and non-tangibles—clothing, cubicles, rules, hierarchies, time constraints.

While some like structure, having to answer to an alarm clock might be difficult, as many people with AS have difficulty keeping regular sleeping hours. The clothing they might be expected to wear (e.g. a suit and tie) may be unnatural and uncomfortable; many like the feel of natural fabrics and/or well-worn items, and do most of their shopping at thrift stores. Having to be somewhere at a specific time and performing according to others' expectations can put pressure on them and create a paralysis of will.

Because many people with AS are highly intelligent, they may have a hard time with teachers that are not up to par in their eyes, and bosses that don't run things as well as they could. If they don't quit because of any of the above, the know-it-all nature of an intelligent Aspie has been known to upset a few bosses here and there, causing termination of employment.

As a result, many have gone through a series of jobs

and have had unsatisfactory experiences which get more discouraging as the years pass. This may test your respect for your AS man and make you question his abilities. Even if it doesn't, it might still be a source of frustration, pain, and financial worries for both of you.

Many people with AS learn to be self-reliant because they realized long ago that they were a foreigner in a strange land. They got used to rejection and not fitting in. (This may partly explain the reluctance or mistrust of the whole relationship idea in the first place.)

HIS WORDS

"Why pay for college, when I can learn that stuff in the library for free?"

"I'd find fault with almost any boss."

"I had a problem with some of the clothing, especially the tie and the shoes."

"My perfect boss would look, sound, and think like me. Actually my perfect boss would be me."

WHAT TO DO

Support him in his quest for education and financial stability. There is support out there (although perhaps not enough yet) that might assist him in hanging on. If he manages to make it through to a doctoral study, he will probably be happiest with that phase of his education, having more autonomy. And certain jobs will be better than others—there are books and lists out there of jobs that are more appropriate for people with AS. If he really cannot function in a social environment, then discuss with him alternative ways—distance learning, self-employment, and so on.

THE POSITIVE NOTE

The self-sufficiency they acquire have led many people with AS to start their own business or become innovators in their field. It is hoped that your AS man has learnt to trust and respect his own original thinking on many matters. Temple Grandin is a fine example of someone with AS who listened to her own voice and despite being ostracized by her coworkers, eventually won their respect and changed the way that some animal-handling businesses were run (2006). There are probably many thousands who, while perhaps not so well-known (at least not for having AS), have done marvelous things and acquired fame, wealth, and respect for their innovative visions.

11

He may get depressed
and/or be completely
inert for long periods
of time

Whether he's just watching television, surfing online, or sleeping odd/long hours, your man may do it with an almost inhuman dedication. Although it sounds quite Zen, it can be more than a bit frustrating to watch him become one with the television, bed, or computer when there are chores to be done or a world to explore.

The Asperger mind works at a mile a minute. It is always thinking, computing, trying to figure things out. Immersing oneself in a mindless or repetitious activity can be a way of turning off the mind and recharging his battery.

Some with AS say that their mind and body involuntarily "shut down" after too much social contact, pressure, or overstimulation. The consensus is that this is an unpleasant and unwelcome state.

This is probably one of his reasons for not wanting to cohabitate or get too close to another. He knows that he is excessive in his "lazy activities." He knows there will be times he shuts down. He probably was criticized by his parents or previous girlfriends for it and believes you will probably take issue with it as well. He needs to be alone sometimes, away from prying eyes. Cohabitation means he may never feel as relaxed as he needs to be. This relaxation, this cocooning, is absolutely essential to a person with AS.

Depression is a side effect of Asperger's. If his inertia is due to depression, he probably needs something he's not getting, and as his friend, you might want to find out what it is. That may be difficult as he won't want to tell you outright, or he may not know himself.

HIS WORDS

"I am very patient and never angry. But I'm very passive. I can lay on the couch watching TV for an entire day and be perfectly happy. I know this bothers her but I can't help it."

"When I'm depressed I just want to be alone. I get over it eventually."

"When my mom yelled at me, I would go in my room and lie on my bed. I couldn't move or speak."

WHAT TO DO

Although some doctors prescribe medications for the depression, inertia, and anxiety that often accompany AS, it will only be a temporary fix. The best thing you can do is to try and encourage or support (but don't push) him to do the things he finds rewarding. Do not nag him or criticize him for being lazy. You'll have to take the reins when it comes to seeing a play, booking a vacation, or going for an autumn drive. Organizing these kinds of social activities are not an Aspie's forte. As for yourself, you will again have to practice your now saint-like patience and keep busy enough to not let it bother you so much.

THE POSITIVE NOTE

At least he can relax, which is probably the opposite of what he is when he is working and engaged.

12

There will be times
he embarrasses you

AS folks can have what I call "singing frog syndrome." Have you ever seen that famous old cartoon where a man discovers a singing, dancing frog? He excitedly takes it to a vaudeville theater and puts it on the stage with a top hat and cane, expecting it to dazzle everyone else as well. To his dismay it just sits there croaking like a typical frog. Most women will report being impressed by the intellect and sex appeal of their AS man, and then when they bring him out to meet their family and friends, he closes up, and/or acts very strangely. This may embarrass you, and make you wonder if you imagined his personality was completely different. You didn't. He has impaired social interaction and social withdrawal, perhaps not all the time, but most likely when he's feeling scrutinized, pressured, or conscious of expectations. You might not notice this until the first time you are out among other people.

He can be clumsy. You may find, once the blinkers of new love are off (or even sooner), that he walks funny—doesn't swing his arms at all, or swings them too much. He may drag his feet, or run like he's skating on ice. He may raise his eyebrows a lot in a worried expression, or have some of the more evident physical signs of AS—rocking, etc. In photographs he may look stunned and uncomfortable, like a deer caught in headlights. He may knock things over at the dinner table and spill half his food down the front of his shirt. He may wipe his mouth on his sleeve or wear his clothes inside out. Chances are, you'll probably notice and mind it more than anyone else will.

His rudeness may be another source of embarrassment. Not shaking hands with men he's introduced to and not saying goodbye when you leave functions. Bringing a newspaper to read at a formal wedding reception. He doesn't mean to be rude, most likely, but is just extremely uncomfortable. His gruffness, if he is gruff, is just masking his discomfort; he's either pretending he doesn't care or has given up trying.

HIS WORDS

"First impressions don't mean anything. It's easy to impress someone at first but after you get to know them or they get to know you, it's easy to have contempt."

"I'm alright for a while and then I have to leave because I get in a bad mood."

"It's easier to small talk with strangers. It gets harder for me when I have to be with people hour after hour, week after week; then my social difficulties become more pronounced."

"Repressing my physical tics damaged me."

"I didn't know I walked funny till my best friend told me. Then I stopped swinging my arms like that."

WHAT TO DO

First of all, some of the physical things can be unlearnt. You have to decide if something bothers you enough to mention it, or if it's causing problems for your man, and you truly want to tell him for his own sake. Be gentle about it. He probably has no idea he's doing it and will be horrified that no one's told him before. If his behavior is embarrassing to you, is it about you and your pride, or is it about protecting him? You may have to tell family and friends the cause of his sometimes quirky behavior in order to have their understanding. They might not even notice it, but because you want to make a good impression, you are super-conscious of it.

You need to search within yourself and see how much appearances and social conventions mean to you. If they mean a lot, dating an Aspie is going to be a bigger challenge for you than if they don't.

THE POSITIVE NOTE

You may become less superficial and concerned with what others think.

13

Your family and friends
may think you're being
a doormat and a fool

Your loved ones probably just want you to be happy. When they see how hard you have to work at your relationship, especially if the effort exceeds the reward, your family and friends will likely think you're selling yourself short. They may feel that he doesn't deserve you, especially if they haven't taken the time to learn about AS. Many of *his* family members will probably feel similarly, so at least you'll have their sympathy. As a matter of fact, you'll probably get more understanding from his family than your own, because they have had to deal with his behavior for a long time and know what a struggle it can be. This can sustain you emotionally in hard times, but it won't replace having a partner who is there for you 100 percent.

Consider, too, that they may have a point. Maybe you are not being treated as well as he could treat you—AS is not an excuse to abuse. Try to remember also, that if they are judging your relationship negatively based on what you tell them, you must be complaining, perhaps more than you realize.

It can be hard to explain to those who've never been in a relationship with a man with AS, just how wonderful they can be, and how they simply cannot have the same emotional responses as an NT man. Don't expect your family and friends to fully understand. It won't help if they constantly "nay-say" your relationship, or always take your side, for that will just reinforce the negative thoughts in your mind. On the other hand, you don't want them to always take his side either, because that invalidates your feelings. You may not be able to count on them for impartial, constructive advice.

HIS MOTHER'S WORDS

"When he was little the doctor told me he was ADHD and put him on Ritalin. I took him off after one week because I knew that wasn't right. I couldn't handle him when he was growing up. He can be the sweetest guy in the whole entire world but then sometimes he can be infuriating. I love him but he still drives me crazy."

WHAT TO DO

Let them know that, although things can improve, it may take some time and effort. Understanding the cause of negative behavior does not mean condoning it. Ask friends and family to educate your man by their own example. People with Asperger's are good emulators, and if they see a healthy relationship and healthy ways of being in the world, they will pick up some of these behaviors.

Find a non-biased, non-judgmental listener who isn't just going to take your side, but will try to work with you to figure things out. A counselor who is well-versed in Asperger's syndrome and the impact it can have on a person's life and relationships would be best. The right listener is extremely important, especially if CAD seems to be setting in.

THE POSITIVE NOTE

Friends and family might make you realize just how unhappy you are, and mirror back to you your own words and emotional state. This can be a good indicator of the state of your relationship and is a catalyst for seeking help.

14

People will tell you
he's just being a man

No matter how much they love you, people, especially females, will tell you he's "just being a guy" and you're being oversensitive. That's because their own men do some of the same things that your Aspie does. They don't realize the sweeping scale of the problem. Not being believed is a catalyst for Cassandra Affective Disorder—self-doubt can set in, sabotaging your self-esteem and good mental health. You will begin to wonder if you're just being hypersensitive and imagining that he has a problem. You may begin to blame yourself for all the problems in the relationship.

Note: Many people with AS are undiagnosed, or are first unofficially "diagnosed" by their partner, the one who knows them the most intimately. If your AS male has not received a doctor's official diagnosis, then your burden will be even greater. Your friends will likely doubt your ability to properly identify the cause of his behavior. Of course it would be better for all if he did receive an official verdict, but that is often difficult, sometimes impossible. He may not have health insurance and even if he does, adult diagnosis is difficult to procure in many parts of the USA where the emphasis is on children. The cost can be prohibitively high without insurance. Or he may refuse to go to a doctor. If Asperger's syndrome truly is the framework that seems to fit his behavior, if it helps you deal, if he agrees it seems to make sense, then use the knowledge to your benefit. That is all you can do.

HIS WORDS

"Aspies, although we can seem effeminate, are really very male. We take male qualities to the extreme— the independence, the stoic behavior, lack of emotion and caring."

WHAT TO DO

Nip their disbelief, condescension, doubt, and comparisons with their own husbands in the bud. Tell them they don't know what they are talking about, and that what they are saying to you can be detrimental to your own good mental health. Give them things to read about AS, and introduce them to films and documentaries on the subject. Try to educate them about the world of AS and Cassandra Affective Disorder.

THE POSITIVE NOTE

Even though they are underestimating the scope of his behavior, it can be helpful to be reminded that "normal" men aren't perfect either—and no relationship is.

3

Labels and romantic
expectations make
him feel nervous

Some women find that just calling him their "boyfriend" can make him sweat bullets. Saying "I love you" can leave him feeling positively smothered. While some AS males are comfortable with the "L" word, others are not. If yours isn't, you may be better off never saying it. Even if he doesn't mind hearing it, he might never say it back—AS males are more comfortable demonstrating their feelings through actions, not words. This can be tough to handle; at some point, most women need to hear "I love you."

Speaking of expectations, don't assume he will honor birthdays, Christmas, or anything else. He will say things like "Tell me what you want" because he can't guess. If you tell him nothing, that is exactly what you'll get.

HIS WORDS

"I show my love in lots of little ways. Anyone can say I love you. It doesn't mean they mean it."

"I could never say it to my mom and now I can't say it to my girlfriend."

WHAT TO DO

Some women say they have "trained" their male to say "I love you" on occasion, but most agree he seems uncomfortable with it. A little compromise goes a long way, but definitely look at his actions more than his words. As stated elsewhere in this book, an AS male will show his love in a myriad of ways that you may not even notice. The old adage "You don't know what you've got till it's gone," can apply here. If you take a bird's eye view of your relationship, does he show his love in other ways?

15

You must have a good social
support network so you can
go out and have fun
once in a while

By good social support I am not talking about calling your mom or best friend and having a good moan about your relationship. It's important that you have friends that you go out with on a regular basis, so you can have fun, let loose, and de-stress. Laughing and joking can be rarities in Aspie relationships, and even if they're not, you probably don't see him that often and it's not healthy for anyone to spend too much time alone. Having a social life apart from him will help you to give him some space, without being lonely yourself.

He may encourage you to go out with friends, even other guys. Unless he's pushing you out of a relationship, he doesn't mean he wants you to sleep with other men, just take some of the pressure off him to be your whole world.

HIS WORDS

"My girlfriend doesn't have enough friends and I don't like that. She relies on me too much for everything."

"I learn a lot from my female friends and I don't want to lose them just because I'm in a relationship."

WHAT TO DO

Make a conscious effort to do things without him. Even if you don't want to.

THE POSITIVE NOTE

This will force you to do what a lot of people know they should do, but often don't—Keep Your Friends!

16

Your AS male will not care
about the things you do
without him and there will
be things he does not
share with you

If you are involved in something that is exciting and ful-filling for you, he may not want to hear about it. He might cut you off, change the subject, or leave the room while you're in mid-sentence. He might never ask about your work, except in the most practical of ways. He won't want to know about your inner life. He's too wrapped up in his own. This can be frustrating to say the least.

When he first met you or when he meets someone new, he will take a keen interest and listen intently; this is part of his charm. But as soon as he feels he knows all there is to know about a person or topic, and has decided it is not someone or something which interests him, he can be quite rude. His disinterest also has to do with taking you for granted and with not wanting to be your whole world. It is alright with him if he is not. Compartmentalizing is something people with AS do well—he may have activi-ties he enjoys and friends he hangs out with, and never invite you along. He may not want to jeopardize things that are working just fine as they are. If he has a recipe for success in an area of his life, adding a new ingredient (you) would be unwise.

A WORD OF CAUTION

An AS male may keep his relationship with you completely separate from his friends, your friends, and everyone else in the world. As a result, you may have few witnesses to your love. This isolation is dangerous. It means you will have no observers to anything that occurs—the good or the bad. This is throwing wide the door for Cassandra Affective Disorder. Also, what I mentioned earlier applies—people with AS are good actors. His "regular" friends may not have a clue as to what he's like in a relationship and may not even know he has Asperger's. They may think that he's a lone wolf, eccentric, quirky, effeminate, etc., all sorts of things, but few will know or believe that he can be cruel, even unintentionally. He could, theoretically, treat you abominably and never be told by anyone he cares about that he behaved badly.

WHAT TO DO

Try to get him to take turns talking and listening when you do meet. Ask him how his day was, and then tell him about yours. If he ignores what you say, gently remind him that you listened to him talk about his day, and that this is what people do for one another. The best thing you can do is keep talking anyway; he may learn to listen. Over time, he'll become educated in a topic that was previously outside his realm of experience. It may become something that is of interest to him, strengthening your bond. And if it doesn't ... keep your own interests. If you write, join a writer's club. If you read, join a book club. If you sing, join a choir or a band, and so on. Do not put your own life on hold because you get so wrapped up in your partner's interests.

Do try to have mutual friends and don't let your relationship exist in a vacuum. But be aware that jealousy and possessiveness do not fly with an AS male. Try to let him feel free to do as he pleases as long as he is not hurting anything other than your pride.

THE POSITIVE NOTE

You will retain some of the mystery that all men find so alluring if you do things that don't include him. And, you will feel more fulfilled if you follow pursuits that hold meaning for you.

17

Time holds a different
meaning for him than
it does for you

It's not unusual for a person with AS to say "I'll be right over," and then not arrive for many hours. They can get caught up in things along the way—phone calls, shopping, etc. A video store is a sand-trap; it can easily hold the attention of an Aspie for an hour or more, where most NTs would be in and out in a few minutes. Your man may arrive triumphantly, five DVDs in hand, not realizing that it is past your bedtime and too late to watch one anyway. You may be tapping your fingers on the dining room table, watching dinner get cold; meanwhile he is at his house catching up on paperwork because he didn't think the exact time was important. If you have an appointment to meet somewhere, he'll probably be on time, but if it's a casual thing, he may not realize that he is inconveniencing you by being late. He would probably not be upset if you were late and assumes you would feel the same way. He won't know unless you tell him.

He also may not call you for days without realizing just how much time has passed.

HIS WORDS

"If I invited you over for a movie and you were late, I would find plenty of things to do until you arrived."

"Is it that late?"

WHAT TO DO

Don't be offended. Just try to explain that your time is valuable to you and you don't like to be left hanging; that if he is going to be late he should call. If you don't hear

from him for a while, go ahead and ring him. Unless he's
gone cold on the relationship, he'll be glad you did.

THE POSITIVE NOTE

You may acquire more patience than you ever thought
possible. You may discover creative ways to fill your own
time with meaningful activities.

18

He may want to sleep on
the couch starting very early
in the relationship and
continuing throughout

This can happen even if your sex life is adequate or better. It can also happen whether you live together or not. You will feel rejected and confused. It is not you—he may be very sensitive physically and emotionally and sometimes needs to sleep alone.

If you do touch him while he's asleep, even inadvertently, he can react violently. He will not be fully awake while doing so. Women have been elbowed in the back and pushed out of bed. He may steal the covers or refuse to share them with you outright. His rationale is that he needs a good night's sleep, and may have little concern for yours. Some AS men keep their own separate room, or even have a separate house, apartment, boat, etc., just so they can have their own guaranteed space. Your man may need this indefinitely.

This also relates to the need for solitude and physical comfort mentioned earlier. We all like to be comfortable but it is taken to a higher level when one has Asperger's. His pajamas and sheets will have to be made of certain materials, and your night clothes as well if he's to sleep with you.

Meanwhile, as he's snoring away on the couch or at the far end of your queen-size bed, you may lose a lot of sleep wondering what it is you're doing wrong; why you displease or bore him. Provided you are fairly even-tempered and rational, it's not you, it's Asperger's.

HIS WORDS

"Beds are for sex and sleeping, not for cuddling."

"Most of the time, I'm not comfortable with people touching me. It makes me very jumpy and twitchy."

WHAT TO DO

There can be compromises made, for example that he is only to sleep on the couch twice a week instead of every night. You can try and see if he'll go for it. Make it an official contract, and offer something in exchange, since he'll believe it is a big sacrifice on his part.

Don't use alcohol, sleeping pills, or other drugs to get your rest. Instead try to seek help and keep a perspective on things. Learn other more constructive ways to get some shut-eye—yoga, meditation, relaxation techniques, etc. There are also non-addictive natural sleep aids like chamomile tea, lavender, and melatonin tablets.

THE POSITIVE NOTE

You will often have that big ol' bed to yourself. You might even have time to write your own book during those restless nights! (How do you think I managed this one?)

19

You will never change him,
even if you can succeed
in getting him to change
his behavior

AS is not treatable. There are no drugs and no cures, although some doctors will prescribe medications for the anxiety and depression that often accompanies AS. But merely receiving the diagnosis may give him a fresh perspective and motivation, a sense of freedom and relief. Through therapy and counseling your AS male can learn that there are ways to behave that will ultimately benefit both him and you.

As for whether or not it is a good idea to be with someone whom you even want to change, well, there are two points of view to this one. Since the behavior of an AS male often fluctuates drastically, it's only natural that you would prefer to see more of his considerate, positive, affectionate side and less of the "cold and negative." As for what the males themselves prefer, some say they are most comfortable with someone who accepts them exactly as they are, while others will tell you they chose their partner because she challenged him to grow and change. (As for what type of challenges, they might mean physical rather than emotional challenges, like trying kung fu as opposed to talking about feelings.)

He may disagree with many of the points in this book, or he may agree with them but not understand what the big deal is. So even if he does read this and other books, you are not going to see a drastic transformation, at least not overnight.

HIS WORDS

"If I want to keep a girl in my life I will compromise. If I don't I probably won't."

"Asperger's is just another thing like restless leg syndrome."

WHAT TO DO

Ask yourself how much you really want to change him. Despite the frustration, there any many gifts that come with AS. The very things that drive you nuts might be inherently intertwined with the things that are most beguiling.

THE POSITIVE NOTE

We usually get who and what we need at the time, even if the meaning and reason is well hidden from us.

20

Even if he loves you and
values your relationship, it
is possible you may never
get a commitment

He may outright declare that marriage will "never" happen, even if he says he can't imagine being with anyone but you. This announcement may come early on, or later, after a lot of time and effort on your part to create a healthy relationship and make him happy. It might not even be announced verbally, it might be more of a sudden, silent revelation. This can feel like you've been putting money into a savings account and then, when you need it most, you find out it is empty.

Emotions are processed differently by those with AS, and your male may approach love as analytically as he approaches everything else. Think about how he shops. Chances are, he researches a product in depth and compares prices long before he buys. He would probably like to do this with women as well, but because of his social phobias, won't get the chance to. His shyness will prevent it. So when he is with a woman, he may feel that he didn't give others enough of a chance, and may hesitate to "buy" (i.e. marry or commit). He may question you as to how you can possibly know he's the right one for you, not being able to fathom that sort of decisiveness on such an important issue.

He might be concerned that the personal and social expectations of marriage will put undue pressure on him and on your relationship. If he likes things the way they are, he may feel "if it ain't broke don't fix it."

He may also have low self-esteem and worry that he is not capable of making a good husband, financially, emotionally, or socially.

Family examples and past experiences will leave an indelible mark. If his parents are happily married he will probably accept the possibility of such a thing occurring. If his parents divorced, he may view marriage with a "Why?" rather than "Why not?"

If you were married to another and divorced, he may also take that as an inevitability in all your relationships, including the one you share with him.

Some men, AS and otherwise, have married out of compliance, because that is what they thought they should do, and are in the marriage half-heartedly. You probably would not want that.

HIS WORDS

"I'm not afraid of marriage, I'm afraid of divorce and losing my children. That's why I'll probably never get married or have kids."

"If a woman is willing to spend the rest of her life with an Aspie, because he has low self-esteem, he might think there's something wrong with her."

"I'm married, and just had the usual wedding-day nerves. I was never afraid of it."

WHAT TO DO

No two men with AS are exactly alike and some do marry, and marry successfully. If he is not the marrying kind, only you can decide if you can live with that.

THE POSITIVE NOTE

Marriage can and does often put pressure on people, and he wouldn't be the first to question whether or not it is necessary. You obviously are not too attracted to the conventional, or you wouldn't be in a relationship with this man in the first place.

21

Many AS/NT relationships
go through various
metamorphoses

You may date first, then break up as you realize he has behavioral problems. You may become friends and then go back to dating again. This can happen again and again. Because Aspies are more comfortable with old friends than new, they may return to an old lover more readily than an NT male. The downside of that is that if they (and/ or you) haven't changed, whatever made you break up the first time (or third, or tenth) will still be there. Also, once a certain level of trust has been severely breached and has left that indelible mark it may be next to impossible to mend the rift between you.

He may never love you as much as you love him, or in quite the same way. Of course a man with AS can love, but very often it is difficult to tell what *type* of love they feel for you, and just how deeply. Some AS males say they have never been in love; that they don't think they can feel such feelings. Generally, all of them acknowledge that it's good to have companionship but agree that it creates stress. The more a woman "demands" that he comply with her wishes, to her idea of partnership, the more it validates his thinking that relationships are more bother than they are worth.

If you do the leaving, be warned. It is never easy to leave someone you love, no matter how difficult it was. The good things will come to mind. If he leaves you, he probably won't feel nearly as bad about it as you do. As mentioned, there does seem to be a "disconnect" that goes on, usually temporary, between the heart and mind of a person with AS. You might be devastated and con-fused while he's looking ahead and not missing you in the slightest. To be left this way by a man you've worked so hard to keep happy can leave you with bitterness and regret, anger and desperation. Chances are, he never made any promises unless you were married. If he didn't say it explicitly, then in his mind, it didn't happen. He can't read between the lines and wouldn't expect you to. Still, that doesn't make it any easier.

The romantic part of your relationship may not be meant to be for ever. (For some it is never on the cards.) I don't want to sound like I believe that people with AS cannot be in successful long-term relationships. They can. It happens all the time. But, for your own sake, try to have realistic expectations and keep an open mind to possibilities.

HIS WORDS

"When we split up, I fooled around with plenty of girls but then I went back to her. It can get really lonely without a steady, loving partner."

"I knew she loved me, and I wanted to love her but I just didn't feel it. A year or two later she married someone else. I'm not jealous, I'm happy for her."

"I knew she missed me like crazy but I didn't care. Then one day I did miss her. We got back together and we will probably be together for a while."

WHAT TO DO

As stated earlier, AS males are more comfortable demonstrating their feelings through actions, not words. Demanding to know how much he loves you may lead you to hear things you don't want to hear. You may find that he doesn't love you as much as you thought. If that is the case, you must decide what to do. Relationships should be

50/50 (some say 100/100), and the strain on you might be too much over time.

I know from experience just how passionately we can love our AS men. Just be careful, be positive, and be as protective of your own heart as you are of his. If he breaks up with you, don't rage at him and at the world, even if it comes as a shock. Realize he is not processing things the way you'd expect. Try to forgive, for your own sake.

THE POSITIVE NOTE

There is something inherently Buddhist in Asperger's syndrome. I've often thought that Buddha himself might have been an Aspie. If you know anything about that philosophy, there is a principle of non-attachment that runs throughout the teachings; the thread that ties it all together. I think the biggest challenge for a woman in a relationship with an AS male, is to practice non-attachment. Non-attachment to outcomes, to expectations, and to a person. As one AS male told me, "no expectations, mean no disappointments." Just as this man liked to treat all people equally regardless of age, gender, etc., and felt everyone should practice this, he believed no one should ever expect anything from anyone else. That sounds either utopian or hellish, depending on your perspective. But certainly there is some wisdom in that man's truth.

If you do break up, for a time, or for for ever, you may find he is a better friend than partner. Being friends may be something you never had a chance to do. Without desire and expectation putting pressure on both of you, compassion and affection for each other may finally have space to grow.

22

Your relationship
will stand a much better
chance if your man will
REACH

REceive an official diagnosis, **A**cknowledge he has Asperger's, **C**ommit to your relationship, and seek **H**elp.

If you are doing the work for two, you will get tired, stressed, and eventually you will burn out. You need to know that you are not the only one keeping the relationship together.

QUESTIONS TO ASK YOURSELF

"Why do we do it?" We sometimes have to ask this question when often there is so little given back. I liken being in a relationship with an AS male to living in a climate where the sun doesn't shine very often. When it does, it is dazzling, and you appreciate it so much more than someone who lives in a place where the sun always shines. You live for those moments of light. With the right help, you can make those moments happen a little more frequently and last a bit longer.

"At what point do I stop using Asperger's syndrome as an excuse for everything, and start requiring some effort and reciprocation from my partner?" AS is a reason, but not an excuse. For a woman in love with an AS male it is so very hard to know when and where to draw the line. Some men and women will be more willing to compromise than others; some may find this dance fairly simple to follow while others trip and fall a few times. Every couple is unique.

"Is this person/relationship really worth all the effort?" That is something only you can answer and will depend entirely upon how much you love him, how compatible you are, and how much consideration you have for one another.

Remember that happiness should be the main ingredient in any relationship, and that you—and he—are as worthy of it as any two people. I hope you both find yours.

GLOSSARY OF TERMS

Asperger's syndrome (AS): an autism spectrum disorder first described by Hans Asperger. It is a milder form of autism, characterized by qualitative impairment in social interaction. This is manifest through impairment in non-verbal behaviors, e.g. eye contact, facial expression, body postures and gestures; failure to develop appropriate peer relationships; lack of social reciprocity; restricted, repetitive patterns of behavior, interests, and activities; inflexible adherence to routines or rituals, and abnormal preoccupations (NCBI 2008).

Aspie: a person with Asperger's syndrome. Not derogatory, but an informal term which is popularly used in forums and self-reference.

Autism Spectrum Disorders (ASD): also known as *pervasive development disorders*. They are characterized by varying degrees of impairment in communication skills, social interactions, and restricted, repetitive, and stereotyped patterns of behavior. They can range from severe autism to Asperger syndrome.

Cassandra Affective Disorder (CAD): CAD was originally conceived in 1998 by FAAAS as the "Mirror Syndrome." Through the years it has been further described and refined by Maxine Aston in England, and by Dr Tony Attwood in Australia. According to Aston (2008), "People with Asperger syndrome emotionally deprive (usually unintentionally) their partners and this, in turn, will have an effect on the mental and physical health of that deprived partner in the relationship. It is especially extreme if the couple are unaware of the cause (AS) of the relationship problems."

***Diagnostic and Statistical Manual of Mental Disorders*, 4th edition (DSM-IV):** a manual published by the American Psychiatric Association that includes all currently recognized mental health disorders. The coding system utilized by the DSM-IV is designed to correspond with codes from the World Health Organization (WHO) *International Classification of Diseases*, commonly referred to as the ICD (Wikipedia 2008).

Neurotypical (NT): although not the strict definition, this is a term often used to describe a person who does not have Asperger's or any other autism spectrum disorder.

RECOMMENDED READING, RESOURCES AND REFERENCES

RECOMMENDED READING

Hawkins, G. (2004) *How to Find Work That Works for People with Asperger Syndrome: The Ultimate Guide for Getting People with Asperger Syndrome into the Workplace (and Keeping Them There!)*. London: Jessica Kingsley Publishers.

Hendrickx, S. and Newton, K. (2007) *Asperger Syndrome—A Love Story*. London: Jessica Kingsley Publishers.

RESOURCES

Rudy Simone's website. Periodic updates on research, books and activities, as well as helpful resources for those with AS, including definitions, lists of symptoms and links. (www.help4aspergers.com)

Website of author Maxine Aston. Maxine provides counseling, assessment, and workshops for those with AS, their partners, and families. (www.maxineaston.co.uk)

REFERENCES

Aston, M. (2005) *Aspergers in Love—Couple Relationships and Family Affairs*. London: Jessica Kingsley Publishers.

Aston, M. (2008) *The Asperger Couple's Workbook: Making Difference Work—Practical Advice and Activities for Couples and Counselors alike*. London: Jessica Kingsley Publishers.

Attwood, T. (2003) *Is There a Difference Between Asperger's Syndrome and High Functioning Autism?* Available at www.sacramentoasis. com/docs/8-22-03/as_&_hfa.pdf, accessed October 20, 2008.

Attwood, T. (2007) *The Complete Guide to Asperger's Syndrome*. London: Jessica Kingsley Publishers.

Barnhill, G. (2004) 'Asperger syndrome: a guide for secondary school principals.' www.nasponline.org/resources/ principals/nassp-asperger.aspx, accessed March 21, 2009.

Fitzgerald, M. and Molyneux, G. (2004) 'Overlap between alexithymia and Asperger's syndrome.' *Am J Psychiatry* 161, 11, 2134–2135.

Grandin, T. (2006) *My Life in Pictures*. New York, NY: Vintage Books.

Lawrence, R. (Producer) and Næss, P. (Director). (2005) *Mozart and the Whale* (Motion picture). USA: Big City Pictures. (Based on the book by Newport, J. Newport M., and Dodd, J.)

National Center for Biotechnology Information (NCBT). *Asperger Syndrome, Susceptibility To, 1*. Available at www.ncbi. nlm.nih.gov/entrez/dispomim.cgi?id=608638, accessed July 27, 2008.

Wikipedia. *DSM-IV Codes*. Available at http://en.wikipedia. org/wiki/DSM-IV_Codes, accessed October 20, 2008.